Venezuelan red howler monkey

White-faced saki

Amazonian umbrellabird

King vulture

Hercules beetle

Common squirrel monkey

Amazonian motmot

Emperor tamarin

South American coati

Harpy eagle

Common vampire bat

Scarlet macaw

Green oropendola

Capuchinbird

Black-bearded saki

One Day on Our Blue Planet … in the Rainforest © Flying Eye Books 2017.

This paperback edition published in 2019. First published in 2017 by Flying Eye Books, an imprint of Nobrow Ltd. 27 Westgate Street, London E8 3RL.

Text and illustrations © Ella Bailey 2017.
Ella Bailey has asserted her right under the Copyright, Designs and Patents Act, 1988, to be identified as the Author and Illustrator of this Work.

1   3   5   7   9   10   8   6   4   2

Published in the US by Nobrow (US) Inc.
Printed in Poland on FSC® certified paper.

ISBN: 978-1-912497-31-7

www.flyingeyebooks.com

Ella Bailey

ONE DAY
ON OUR
BLUE PLANET

...IN THE RAINFOREST

Flying Eye Books

London | New York

As the morning sun rises over the rainforests
of South America, a young black spider monkey
and his mother look out across the treetops.

Relaxing nearby are the rest of his family,
who all live together in a group called a troop.

They use barks and screeches to talk to each other. It can be very noisy!

The little monkey clings tightly to his mother's back. Using her strong tail like an extra arm, she swings through the tangled branches...

...to the strangest and most beautiful birds.

But where has this monkey's mother gone?
He cannot see her anywhere in the crowded canopy.

...reaching for the most delicious fruits and leaves to eat.

The rainforest is home to many other creatures,
from tiny marmosets and tamarins...

He searches through the dense lower levels of the rainforest...

...and emerges above a winding river.

His troop often comes down here to drink, but his mother is nowhere to be found!

He never ventures this far down on his own. The plants
and creatures here have adapted to the low light...

...and not all of them are friendly!

Here she is! Luckily, there are very few things
that can catch a spider monkey in the trees.

Darkness draws in, and the night-time animals begin
to emerge from their hidden nests and secret burrows.

The monkey's mother carries him to the safety
of their troop's favourite sleeping tree.

As the forest buzzes with the sounds of insects,
the little monkey sleeps in his mother's arms...

...until a new sun rises, on another day on our blue planet.

ANIMALS OF THE RAINFOREST
DOWN BELOW

Capybara

Tambaqui

South American tapir

Hoatzin

Ocelot

Amazon kingfisher

Paca

Electric eel

Amazon river dolphin

Jaguar

Tayra